NOT IN VAIN
YOU'VE SENT ME LIGHT

ESSENTIAL POETS SERIES 287

**Canada Council Conseil des Arts
for the Arts du Canada**

**ONTARIO ARTS COUNCIL
CONSEIL DES ARTS DE L'ONTARIO**

Canadä

Guernica Editions Inc. acknowledges the support of the Canada Council
for the Arts and the Ontario Arts Council. The Ontario Arts Council
is an agency of the Government of Ontario.

We acknowledge the financial support of the Government of Canada.

CORA SIRÉ

NOT IN VAIN
YOU'VE SENT ME LIGHT

GUERNICA
EDITIONS

TORONTO – CHICAGO – BUFFALO – LANCASTER (U.K.)
2021

Elana Wolff, editor
Michael Mirolla, general editor
Cover and interior design: Errol F. Richardson
Guernica Editions Inc.
287 Templemead Dr., Hamilton, Ontario, Canada L8W 2W4,
2250 Military Road, Tonawanda, N.Y. 14150-6000 U.S.A.
www.guernicaeditions.com

Distributors:
Independent Publishers Group (IPG)
600 North Pulaski Road, Chicago IL 60624
University of Toronto Press Distribution (UTP)
5201 Dufferin Street, Toronto (ON), Canada M3H 5T8
Gazelle Book Services, White Cross Mills
High Town, Lancaster LA1 4XS U.K.

First edition.
Printed in Canada.

Legal Deposit – First Quarter
Library of Congress Catalog Card Number: 2021930873
Library and Archives Canada Cataloguing in Publication
Title: Not in vain you've sent me light / Cora Siré.
Other titles: Not in vain you have sent me light
Names: Siré, Cora, author.
Series: Essential poets ; 287.
Description: First edition. | Series statement: Essential poets series ; 287 |
Poems.
Identifiers: Canadiana 20210110031 | ISBN 9781771836111 (softcover)
Classification: LCC PS8637.I726 N68 2021 | DDC C811/.6—dc23

Contents

MATCHING SCARS

*To emphasize only the beautiful seems to me
to be like a mathematical system
that only concerns itself with positive numbers.*
—Paul Klee

At Our Book-Scrambled Table

We delve into devices,
pause at intervals,
meet the other's gaze.

Today I'm wearing shades
so he can't read my eyes.

Squinting at the French's
Classic – yolkbright
with a crust of dried
mustard by the plastic spout –

I interrupt his peace
to recite the fine print on the label –
tiny as the footnotes to our marriage
certificate (*Citizenship refers to the country
to which the person owes allegiance* ...)
also not inconsequential.

Me: No gluten, calories or fat.
        What else can you say *that* about?
Him: My kiss?

Across the Condiments

He loathes French's
won't touch the stuff.
Where he grew up
the mustard isn't neon bright
but rusty as the cordillera
zingy on your lips –
a bee sting at first taste.

Picture the boisterous Sunday asado –
a crowded table near bushy coffee plants
bougainvillea in cascades of crimson tangles
sunglassed eyes stinging from wood-burn smoke.

Just 25, a so-called gringa,
thinking I'm in the right place
if an ordinary condiment
sounds *this* expressive.

Me: La mostaza, por favor.
Him: What?

Andean Altitude

That night he's frantic, racing through Salta in a Fiat
while I – delirious on the back seat – fend off
florescent alien-demons attacking me

in blinding explosions of dayglo orange, highlighter pink.
Beyond sick, more like a bad acid trip and I wind up injected
in a hospital bed by a commotion of white coats I can't see.

My senses shot for hours until a nurse strokes my forehead –
seems to be saying heat, mayonnaise, meat, pobrecita, high
altitude, she's so young, and look at the sky in her eyes.

Next shaky morning, I don my shades and carry my sandals
back to the parents' casa, sequestered alone in cama
until he gets a doctor friend to check up on me.

The amigo, a swashbuckler with a horsey smell, takes my racing
pulse, pulls a baggie of what looks like weed from his pocket,
says to counter la puna or altitude ills, it's best to chew a wad.

Me: What are these?
Him: Coca leaves.

Red Calamity

I'm flying
high on speed
       wheesh-shuck
around the arena
size of an indoor pond
to Corey Hart and Cyndi Lauper
playing on the PA.

Don't touch me, he says
all wobbling ankles, shin pads.
Oh yeah? Well take this!
I trace counter-clockwise ovals
       wheesh-shuck
gain momentum
trailing clouds of ice chips
grab my ankles and tuck

(what possessed me
such a show-off and mad
about 3 stinging words)

I'm flying
all wheesh no shuck
an aerodynamic cannonball
shooting velocity, totally
underestimating my kph
frenzied *fuck this* anger-fuelled
euphoria.

Just before the
SMACK
time stops.

A nanosecond inside an H.C. Andersen tale:
easy childhood mostly love/nurture
from parents scarred by
tragedies/war doing their best to
recreate a backyard idyll –
a sandbox by the apple trees
        amid dispossessed relatives
        unaware that yelling for a cat
in Russian will alienate
the neighbourhood.

Magic skates for the girl
holding on to a dad
who did stuff with the kids
and a mom who fed the brain
with bedtime fables –
if you're surrounded by a pack of dogs
fall on your knees, repeat *I'm Cora*
I'm Cora in a friendly voice
or better yet: Pray. God exists
to save you despite the father's
raised eyebrows, shrug
(*where was He in '39?*)
        displaced parents working hard
        to get you to fit in, but how can they
        really? You're always her –
        the little match girl gaping at real
        Canadians from the outside

15

looking in, and here you are all grown
up with a gaucho who says, *Don't touch me!*
Maybe not about to live happily
ever after all, leaving the romantic
holding hands to Sunglasses
              At Night and True Colors to real locals
              circling the arena with old maple wood
              splintering off gritty, puck-scarred walls …

SMACK
head on, my face
takes the impact
fainting.

Frantic, he races
through Montreal in a Honda
ambulance in disguise
up night streets narrowed by snowdrifts
screaming at cars that block
the uphill drive to the Royal Vic
because the Gothic
structure looks most reputable.

I wind up
on a gurney in emerg
blood pouring out of my face
a commotion of white coats
asking questions, talking
concussion, frontal lobe
flashlights peering into my eyes
our combined adrenaline
ramping anxiety into
toxic hysteria.

We're separated
and they ask questions
to ascertain no battering
involved, he freaks out
and calls his sister.

The bleeding's staunched
and hours drip by waiting for some specialist
on call who's at a party.

When the swashbuckler
of a plastic surgeon finally arrives
he lifts my bandage and with champagne breath
declares the wound can't be fixed
There'd be a fold between her eyes.

Next morning Em rushes
up on the first bus from Ottawa,
assesses the calamity, my mother who
never trusted men.

The day off work sofa-bound with Em
engaging me in complex conversations
and memory games with a strangely
Netherlandish theme.

> *Remember Rembrandt's chiaroscuro portraits?*
> *Van Gogh's obsession with Japonaiserie?*

> I speak of *Plum Tree in Blossom*
> bolder than Hiroshige. *Yes, good*
> and then she baits me with tiny Tante Züs –
> *Remember in The Hague?*

Sure, I say, circa 1970, she had long braids
and danced in her slippers around the living room.

I don't confess
the ancient auntie scared me
with her craziness, wanting to prove
my head injury's superficial,
genetics notwithstanding,
the brain more or less intact.

After my mother's gone
he sits by my side
staring me in the eyes —

heartbreaking silence
of a haunted man.

Me: So now we've got matching scars.
Him: But yours is beautiful.

Unbearably Close and Distant

Raised in opposing north/south constellations
where do we intersect? At night in the orbit of desire
the metallic splendour of our haloes plays as song.

All I have to do is kiss the pulsing artery on his neck –
we move from slow to urgency, two lunar spheres
circling planet Us. When he plays the clarinet, green
tarnishes my heart for his hands on her shiny keys,
his lips to her embouchure, the thrust of tango
in his hips. I sit at my piano to overplay their lust –
hands flying in counterpoint to jealousy.

This is our conspiracy, the collision of cosmic
melodies from galaxies so close and distant.

Him: Carlos Gardel's *Mi Buenos Aires querido* – largo.
Me: JS Bach's *Invention No. 13* – con spirito.

Maybe the Condor Heard It All

He's just turned six –
rascally setting off caps,
making slingshots, running
wild in short pants
and sandals on Salta's unpaved streets
among skittering chickens, kittens, ferrets.

Snowy glints from the cordillera reflect
a blanching noonday sun –
up where the condor soars
the immensity of her wingspan
casting shadows on cacti spikes.
Dust stirred up by clip-clop horses
hauling carts of grapefruit.

Hammers strike sheet metal
in his father's workshop,
to the tunes of kitchen window songs,
dishes clattering to chattering voices,
the warnings of cicadas
tsk-tsking in hibiscus trees.

I wasn't born but his telling renders
the calamity present: I'm here
in northern Argentina circa '56
can hear the urgency in his friend's call, *Vení!*
Vení! from the house on the corner
three storeys high – a castle when you're a kid –
Come! Come see Chonga's puppies!

He runs towards Martín's voice,
towards the castle's windmill
pumping precious water from a well.
The German Shepherd mix –
protector of street ragamuffins
jumps up from her pups in a huff.
Chonga – all cocked ears
and bristling granite hairs –
growls low. He pivots
and flees

fast as the Andean wind –
fear chasing his little sandals
the half-block home. When he turns back
(who can blame him?) to measure
the progress of his flight,
Chonga leaps
lifts her paw and swipes his face
with the blades of her claw.
SCHLACK.

A backward
fall – maybe the condor
heard it all – clattering dishes, his
mother screaming in Czech, the
hammering ceases
        tsk tsk tsk …

His father runs from his machines, lifts
his bleeding boy into the Rastrojero
pick-up, screeches down the drive
cursing the damned chickens

in Slovenian and swerves
up the street to the clinic.

Not dead, not even an eye lost
the gash sutured, 8 stitches
into a fold – midpoint above his eyes
to the comforting musicality
of a commotion of white-
frocked Peronistas.

When at last it's established
the boy is more or less intact
the father sighs and shrugs
            he saw worse at Mauthausen,
the mother trembles into action –
asks the muchacha to bake up
her son's favourite apricot cake.

He claims he forgave Chonga
even after her grandson's jaws
snapped his shin when he was 13
and the 10 rounds of rabies shots
in Bolivia resulted from another calamity
involving a deranged cat of equally
mixed origins.

Chonga's mark on his forehead endures –
less ugliness than an apostrophe
that cries of possession
and provenance – the inherited
scars of wartime traumas
we   two mongrels   indirectly bear.

Nights we lie
face to face
I trace the fold, pose
questions,
to make sense of it all –
him, me, Us.

Me: So what's your mother tongue?
Him: I don't know.

Origins of the Blast

Listen carefully, my son: bombs were falling
over Mexico City
but no one even noticed.
　　　　　　　—Roberto Bolaño

I.

Power charges his demons. In plain clothes
they fire at students, burn books. Dissidents

disappear. If they don't like your words, you're dead.
Cordoba, Argentina, '74, eve of the coup d'état.

He ambles out with a friend to watch the film.
Finds himself an extra in the bedlam of a university town.

Tear gas, shots and Molotovs. Runs for his life.
Maybe that's when he knows it's too hot

time to leave. No, it was '76, the shattering
aftermath: habeas corpus suspended under martial law.

II.

Yet I'm the one afraid of packs of bared-teeth dogs,
the noisy dark, witches in my bedroom closet, monsters

in my head. If I don't pay attention, meld in, I'm dead.
A real scaredy-cat, all the love can't render me safe.

A hot night in the McGill ghetto, a man tries to climb
into my bedroom window. I'm lying there reading Rilke

"The Song of The Waif" and see him perched on the sill
my neighbour from the first floor, a quiet soul, high as a star.

Teetering, his crazed eyes startle me out of *I am nobody
and always will be*. I flee my apartment

bang on the third-floor doors. Nobody answers. Fly
down stairs barefoot in my T-shirt. Someone calls the police.

Did you recognize the intruder?
How could I denounce him? He isn't the monster

inside my head. I sleep at a friend's, move out Canada
Day '81. Some still believe I imagined the scene

except, years later, him. I didn't know him then
but he lived a block away in a fancier bunker,

La Cité, my friends later call – to taunt me –
bastion of the bourgeoisie.

III.

Delusions parade as illusions. Montreal safe?
Martial law could never happen here?

I witnessed army boys, shiny bayonets on rifles
guarding McGregor (now Dr. Penfield)

the street known as embassy row. Nights
the girls in my boarding school

leaned out the windows to bait them. *Psst* ...,
a flirty game to get the boys to smile

while blocks away, innocents were herded
into makeshift detention – the PVM garage –

arrested for imaginary crimes like possessing
a book on Cubist art. War Measures in '70

suspended habeas corpus. Do away
with 'you should have the body'

is the opening salvo to terror.
Argentina's junta got away with murder –

enabled by the same legal sleight
of hand easily enacted here.

Before Bolaño, I never thought of poets
as detectives who track

collateral damage when fear
is twisted by malicious hands.

IV.

What steely nerves our fathers had. We inherit their terror
but they don't bequeath us their courage. For that we need

forensic verse, read undercover late at night, words
that can be sung or hollered in the language of necessity

at demons charged by power
who keep coming back.

One night my father aged 20 infiltrates
enemy lines, hand on the revolver in his pocket,

speaking Russian to get food
on his flight towards Denmark.

By bonfired encampments, in the shadows of ruins
and mangled materiel, the Soviet officer throws him

a loaf of bread. My father fakes his way
now Russian, now German, now Polish.

He never tells me this story but I overhear him telling
my brother, *that's what fitting in means, son. Survival.*

My beloved's father spends two years hauling
and shattering stones in Mauthausen until

without warning or explanation, he's shoved
on a train. His wife and daughter wait at the Italian border

and when he hobbles off, they don't recognize him.
Wrecked and starved, he survives the charge of treason

for resisting Ljubljana's Nazi occupation.
No luxury for therapy and recovery

he works in Milano, witnesses Mussolini
swinging dead by the piazza.

Our fathers could not believe in God. They'd seen
too much. They held onto love and we were born

after dangerous seaborne journeys, strong mothers
shielding us from their night sweats, screams,

outbursts, erratic behaviour. The paternal shadows cast
speak of differentiation. Fears and paranoia haunt us separately.

V.

We seek cover from missiles the other can't hear
but never question the origins of the blast –

his plain-clothed demons, the monsters
in my head. We tend to the other's cracked

eardrums. Me: What's that sound?
He gets out of bed,

grabs a golf club,
swings at the black.

Diligence

Oh, the foggy decades, two marionettes yanked
through dry-ice haze and corporate agency
as titled wolves connive to pull our strings.

His lair lies underground in fiery furnaces
while mine high-rises out of PowerPoints and briefings.
I envy his tangible outputs – hrs w/o an accident, tons refined/day.

My glories hinge on working capital
backed by camouflage and numbers games.

Friday night, floor 46 in the slate ghost-tower,
my puppet-masters delegate an urgency,
leave me to sweat alone. Zero hour
my 5-line desk phone pulsates.

Him: What the hell are you doing?
Me: Two more hours and I'll be home.

Marriage Certificate Erasure

Ontario certified
and a true statement:
> *marriage answers to place*
> *never religious denomination*
> *or citizenship.*

Place x in proper
square. Birthplace answers to
Fathers   Mothers
Estonia   Estonia
Yugoslavia   Czechoslovakia.

Witness address, parties and
set out to certify peace.

No person shall solemnize
unless duly authorized.

Allegiance
rights of citizenship
license Unitarian space.

Correctness
and sufficiency
not valid.

Marriage Act
April   April
April 9, 1988.

Him: Will this change Us?
Me: I do ... I do not ... I do not know.

Cobalt Is to Red

As races is to flows
As clarinet is to piano
As slingshot is to Frisbee
As explodes is to clams up
As elemental is to metaphoric
As Jacques Tati is to Jerry Lewis
As Catholicism is to confusionism
As el Gaucho de Güemes is to Batman
As Señor Sabelotodo is to Ms. Know-It-All
As heart-on-sleeve is to heart-in-secret-pocket
As Salsa Piri Piri is to French's Classic Mustard

Red on Red

After Mark Rothko's Untitled (Red on Red), *1969*

First glance: an exquisite perfection.
Two squares, each self-contained,
identities in balance, their pasts
assimilated to a present whole. One
resonates scarlet in a choir of joy
while below, ruby red transmits her
cantata of melancholic longing.
Across slim borders, separated only
by fine slices of light, they bleed into
each other. Scarlet seeps into ruby—

a fierce internal argument painted
months before the artist's suicide.
Look deeply: Love and life collide
with fear and death. One is
meaningless without the other, both
trapped in a frameless conversation
from which there's no escaping
scarlet's cries, "Oh, the ecstasy of
existence," and ruby red's replies,
"My love, it is too lonely. I must go."

LISTEN, HEART

... Every *written word is a suicide note.*
And a love letter, too.
—Robert Thomas

Note to a Mapless Self

When wiry springs resist
your bounce and dagger days
of jealousy, indifference
weaken and diffuse, reach
back to good old Wordsworth
wild, eccentric and bizarre
who sometimes got it right:
Heaven lies about us in our infancy!

The trick's to be pre-emptive,
sharp and self-aware.
Take an axe to angst
your clingy friend, taste
magic in the air, read
your Blake to vault rejection.
Whether in Heav'n ye wander fair,
laugh lonely at your inside jokes,
borrow from Japanese poetics,
get who on earth you are.

Eliot was full of it:
I shall not want Honour in Heaven.
Of course you will!
Take flight you trampoliner, dare
to tumble, somersault, ·
vault bluewards and be true
to Pushkin's promise to the angel:
Not in vain you've sent me light.

Go into the Dark

                         and light your candle.
Draw near to focus on the flame.
Sit in stillness. Internalize and concentrate.

Wait until hallucinations, your shadows playing hide
and seek, melt into obscurity. Now squeeze a pinch –
your softest part, the skin of your inner arm, say –

and break the flesh. The pain is sharp yet fleeting,
the wound a reminder of existence. So
you survived. Now go further, grab a chunk –

the cerebral with the coronary – wrench it out.
Bleed. Examine. Share. *Here's the best of me. Careful!*
It's hot as liquid wax

but yours to shape for now.
Love, the giving over
until the snuffing out.

Mirror Princess

After For a Romantic Fantasy
an installation by Stephanie Loveless, Fonderie Darling

some
twirl in the mirror
a pink blur
flash of tiara

some day
one little
girl might look into
the mirror to sing

some day my –
and stop
midway to wonder who
she's really yearning for

some day my prince
or isn't it her pretty
mirrored self

some day my prince will
dismount to
plant a pink lipstick kiss

some day my prince will come
in a bed while she's turned her head
knowing it's the mirror princess
she really truly wants

Confection

Listen.
Listen to the song here
In my heart ...
—Beyoncé from "You Should Have Listened"

In the Christmas concert
at the local Broadway Music
Academy she's on third
tippity-taps into the spotlight
neither tentative nor cocky
in her cherry red heels and
matching rose-print taffeta.

When she belts out
the opening lines
you are star struck
by her kitschy cuteness
how she admonishes
the audience with her outstretched
hand and wags her tiny index finger
You should have listened
at her parents in the front row
geared-up with phones
and selfie sticks aimed at her.

This three-year-old sings
of heartache with such defiance
her cuteness segues into pretend

41

adult-ness. Come to think
of her glued-on eyelashes
she does seem an awful
lot like that murdered beauty-
contestant-child.
              You should have listened

What was her name?
Grasping at lip gloss until
halfway through you almost wreck
her act and yell out
JonBenét Ramsey!!!
just as this little one's life fizzles
inside you, the coming decade
of performance and daughterly duties
followed by frivolous rebellion
or possibly stardom or some
lethal cocktail of the two:
meltdowns, rehab, police line-ups
the rouged shards of her heart
              You should have listened

by which time you'll have aged
as brittle as a swizzle stick while she
ever the cream puff
considers plastic surgery
or at least botox and works
to forgive these two in front of you
who may never grow to ask themselves
what have we wrought?
              You should have listened
to the words when she belted
she was not at home in her home.

A little curtsy, she blows
a kiss and sashays off stage
as the curvy bow of her dress
bobs like a maraschino
about to drown
in the Shirley Temple foam
stirred up in a sugary
faux cocktail.

Doris versus Doris

She's an abomination!
Em declares when we get home
from ballet class and she might as well
have punched me in the gut.

I love Miss Doris
the whole caboodle
of her Saturday morning
classes in the church
basement that's seen
better days but comes
with a piano and
hardwood floors.

Oh, the grace of her, the swish
of her real tutu, red hair swept
up into a beehive bun, her pink lipstick
and sometimes she's just like
I Love Lucy.

Today Miss Doris said,
Be a sunflower!
so we tiptoed in our slippers
to a happy full-of-doo-dah's
Camptown Races song
waving our arms to the pretend
sun in our pink tights and black
leotards and all I could feel

was me shining in a fancy
field of yellow and green.

After I look up abomination
in my big brother's dictionary
I hurl downstairs,
        No she's not!
and Em looks up from her book,
        Then why doesn't she let you
        pick the flower you want to be?

It's like the time I told my mother
I wanted to be Shirley Temple
when I grow up
and Em said that was good
because she's a senator
in the union nations
or something
very upsetting when
you're misunderstood
by your own
mother so I lie,
        I would've picked
        a sunflower anyway
followed by the truth
        Plus she's got the same
        name as you!
to which Em says,
        Unfortunately
while looking down
at the book in her hands
and her voice is too quiet.

Here They Are!

When The Beatles came to Montreal in '64
their landing at Dorval airport was to be broadcast live
on CKGM radio at precisely 3 pm so the big boys
across the street invited neighbourhood kids
to listen in their living room and I was thrilled
because they even invited me.

I didn't know the beetles but imagined a science show
or Magic Tom making the insects disappear or Johnny Jellybean
holding them in his palm while stomping around in his
red and white striped jacket
on noontime TV.

An hour before the show I started to pack my ballet box
because it was music we'd be hearing on the radio
and maybe there'd be dancing!
Then I waited at the front door and when it was 2:55
I took a giant step outside.

Other kids were going into the brick house
across the street with its frayed basketball net
hanging off a wall. Inside, the living room
was really dark and Mrs. D handed out glasses of Kool-Aid
with real ice cubes to a total of 12 kids
jammed on the sofa, lazy boy and footstools.

I sat next to Donnie, drank the green drink
carefully holding my ballet box. When I asked about the dancing
Donnie giggled and his big brother kept saying, *Quiet! Shhh!*
and we had to wait a long time while the kids
were whispering about Paul and John –
not the ones from the Bible: the musicians.

My ice cubes were almost melted
when the announcer yelled HERE THEY ARE!
THE BEATLES ARE IN MONTREAL!
There was screaming like someone got killed
and all the kids in the living room jumped up
and started screaming too.

Mrs. D found me in the corner
and I wasn't really crying
but she walked me home and told Em,
She's just too little for all this,
which was not true! I figured it all out:
Ringo was the best.

The Dial-a-Poem Poets

Please feel free to pretend
the well-heeled junkie
William S. Burroughs
is reciting, his voice
not exciting, very segregation
south, genteel, white male.

Do feel free to imagine
you've redialed up (or down)
and now it's Allen Ginsberg
John Cage or even Patti Smith
as you hold the receiver
(remember that thing?)
to your ear, feverish with rage
that you're here on the island
far from the flower power
and dissent so it's all up
(or down) to little old you
to fight the good fight.

Feel at liberty to say those
were the good old days when
dial-a-poem poets connected moral
imperatives and millions
(not hundreds) showed up
for the showdowns and things
got done, yes they did, things changed.

Feel free to dial up
and have a listen
or better yet buy the album
Sugar, Alcohol & Meat.
Just don't lord your nostalgia
with a gloating lecture on subversion
how we've missed the boat
to redemption – there's much to change
and time (like the poem) is running out.

The Killing Question

Where are you from? she tosses casually,
as in where on earth did you pick up that crazy accent?

To hedge your convoluted past, you state your parents' place of birth.
She's never heard of the distant capital called Tallinn

so she smirks and aims the dart directly at your heart.
Where are *you* from? she follows-up

as if to say in what god-forsaken yard did you once toss
your little ball against a cracked brick wall?

Here, you say, planet earth, same as you,
a last-ditch effort to build some bridge.

Relentless, her impulse to peg and distance
the other, not her or remotely like her.

Where are you from? she asks again
the question that draws blood.

Coming Home

I find a pair of boots –
scuffed, thick-soled
with sturdy laces threaded
through six pairs of eyelets –
in a puddle of melting snow
outside my apartment door.

Inside nobody, not even
behind the shower curtain
or crouching in a closet.
I lift the phone to ask
my mother about the boots
but hang up on the third ring.

There's no point
in trying to call the dead
and you cannot fit
the disappeared
into a single frame to form
a mental photograph.

The Holocaust remains
Norman Mailer
once said in a synagogue
down the street
the thinking man's obsession.

Numbers are an abstraction
until you possess them.
I step inside the unclaimed boots –
the puddle of snow now melted –
and stoop to lace them.

Like a mother's gift
they are a perfect fit.

SINVILLE

Every Bridge Tells a Story

It begins with an acoustic thrum
the segment of a distant sound wave
girding itself for trafficking souls.

Hear heartbeats fluctuate
as steel strings pound
      a mighty span across the waterway
come to the island
cross over
      come home!

How many times have I dared
ride this rollercoaster
once tolled (but free for now)
 up the steel-trussed cantilever?

Returning from Vermont camps
when I still believed in lollipop trees
or from township villages, canton ski slopes,
landlocked fields and *blé d'Inde* stands
to zoom past access points and service roads
congested by tree-felled crescents of developments,
suburban malls with fast food joints to rise
rise upon pre-stressed concrete viaducts
straight on so I don't see the storeys loom
      until I'm actually on the six-lane ramp

funnelling vehicles, motorbikes and megaton
trucks, all of us converging onto the
          arched causeway
in a furious metallic race.

I once had my car crushed on this bridge
as easily as Goliath stomping on a Coke can
so memory collides with terror
in my mental montage of possible disasters
hurtling through space
          to death by drowning
or head-on smash into opposing lanes.
In that roar of velocity,
rubber spinning over asphalt,
rhythmic clicks of equidistant joints
          on the concrete deck –

a story told in heartbeats
I'm transported to
                    the apex
of my vertigo.

Only Canoes Are Smart Enough

Say the crossing's early morning
and the window's open
gee-awk, gee-awk
the bridge defers to back-up songs.

Seagulls – your captains of the St. Laurent –
navigate from upriver Tadoussac
where fresh waters swirl
inside an open seaward mouth.
The birds soar trampled trails
and viaducts to scavenge
on this island inhabited
for 8,000 years –

a span of time sounding
like the rush of white water
parting at the pylons in mid-river
so my fraught nanosecond
on the apex of the old Champlain Bridge
drops quietly
as the dip of a paddle and glides
one droplet in an ancient rippled story.

When Jacques Cartier comes ashore
October 2, 1535
he finds a fortified village
named for the beaver dam and lake –
Hochelaga – home to the Iroquois.

Seven decades on
one Samuel arrives
to find no trace of the village –
its peoples migrated or dead
by imported infectious diseases
and so begins
the occupation.

The Kanien'kehà:ka
call the island Tiohtià:ke
their claim as old as the river,
their mighty highway
forever mutilated by a seaway
flooding the dispossessed
and carved by men
requiring canals to link
great lakes and bypass rocky rapids.
Only canoes are smart enough
        to glide, portage and ride.

Woman of Two Million Names

Her story's told in watery swirls
the foam of shame greased by spill-offs
and refineries to the seasonal crisscross
bleating horns of cruisers and container ships.

If it's night her neon cosmos beckons
lights burlesquing on the river
and beyond
a modest sentry of skyscrapers
guards the escarpment of Mont Royal –
its steel-trussed cross declaring
God is with us
in a baritone voice
belying the complete lack of certitude
required for a leap of faith
of this magnitude to an island
so recently mono-theistically self-identified.

And if it's day I see her renaissance
shrine with its green carapace –
a tiny cross-wingèd thing perched atop –
coming up for air above the maple trees
and city skyline, Twain's clichéd
100 steeples jutting among squat dwellings
erected in some so-called past prosperity,
homes of settlers, immigrants and refugees
busy living old new lives.

Look up, I force myself on the cusp
of our Meccano crossing, *look up
and right at her*
the woman of two million names.

I overhear her beery quarrels
over Montcalm, Wolfe, Harper and PKP
and when I listen deeply, past slot machines'
ka-chíng ka-chíng, tickertape news, hockey scores
talking heads on *Tout le monde en parle,*
I hear the poets sing.

Di Michele dit Brossard dit Dorion
sings Starnino sings Sarah sings Queyras.
*I am the full and unwaning moon for this metro
polis of snow*, says di Michele
*je me tiens infiniment aérienne
avant les questions non loin des rivages*
dit Brossard.
Et Dorion, *Nous descendons,
comme descend le jour, ou le fleuve.*
Says Sarah
*strange things are a-bloom
on Laurier Street*
to which Starnino adds
leaving you lightheaded with revs per thought.
Says Queyras,
If you did not arrive to this city by canoe you can fuck off.

A squatter in layers of leather
and lace, she's of a certain histoire
the life of the party, not shy
to embrace, a sharer of thrills
brutally cold when it suits her
magnetic with a gravity that pulls
me home to flutter my eyelash
on her creased face
and confide to her ear
Je t'adore, Sinville.

HIGH BEAMS

The greatest brightness, short of dazzling, acts near the greatest
darkness.
In this state we at once perceive all the intermediate
gradations of chiaroscuro,
and all the variations of the hues.
—Johann Wolfgang von Goethe, *Theory of Colours*

Somersault

Such beauty's nothing like an arabesque
a lover's sigh   the badass songs of sparrows
the curving breast of an archaic torso
the lonely maple's lucent reds in fall.

Beauty's in her artful eyes   high beams
from the backlit stage   her thrilling seismic sounds
of semiotic mysteries.

It's in the bruises   the charcoal smudge
of shadows beneath her jestful eyes
the mad resilience of her noble hurl
a whirl of prismic colours.   Pride's
the only prize   for having tried.

No net awaits her airborne somersault.
        Such beauty's felt sublime innate.

Rose Juggler

For Su J. Sokol

Inspired inside her tangled petit jardin
she shears a trio of yellow rose stems.

Her bare hands toss and catch one rose then two
and in a deft manoeuvre, left to right hand transfer

she twirls the third and works the rhythms
into a smooth-paced whirl of yellow-green.

She's juggled more than prickly plotlines:
babies, legal briefs and protests, Seders

family apple-picking trips, leaving Brooklyn,
learning French to navigate new interstitial realms.

Today she validates that yes, a lovelorn
character *can* juggle roses, truth cycling

into fiction worthy of each piercing thorn,
her bleeding hands.

Our Critic Toils

Shovel on his shoulder,
he scans vast fields of verse
in search of fertile soil in which to dig.
Rambling in a tract of songetry
he stoops to scoop some home-tilled silt:
Is it common or eclectic, sunbaked
as concrete, wet and wormy or
scattered willy-nilly on the landscape?

He starts to prod. For sweet revenge
let's dissect *his* style: the angle
of his shovel's blade, how sharp its edges
and what vintage – plastic, prone to breakage
or stainless steel – and the mettle he deploys,
the theory to his diggery, the range
and nuance of his grasp whether lyrical
fragmented, measurable in feet or nonce.

Let's eavesdrop on the poetry channel's
live-dig commentary: The pro is focussed
on a patch of stanzas, four octaves tilled
by a compatriot. Blowing snow impedes
his visibility. He aims his shovel, lifts his foot
atop the blade, a muscular down-thrust …
ooh the shovel bounces nastily. He twists the handle,
attacks the soil … aah he nails it smugly.

Our critic toils until a fruitful essay's worth
of clumps and clods have been unearthed,
intentions analysed, soil deconstructed
and demystified leaving the tract exposed
to fertilize. Among his few or many witnesses
there's she who lusts for the cavalry
of poetry police to amass with megaphones:
Drop your shovel, sir, or we'll have to shoot.

Sister

I fall into a strange luminous blindness,
A star, almost a soul, has hidden life from me.
Has it been caught in me like a brilliant butterfly,
Or in its halo of light have I been seized?
　　　　—From "Blindness" by Delmira Agustini
　　　　　　translated from Spanish by Alejandro Cáceres.

In the reflection of your sightless eyes
Dead at 27, the unanswered question
Lies: Was it murder or double suicide?

So the yearning to deduce your eye-rhymed clues
Constructing the elaborate labyrinth
Of your double life. Now you're the specimen

Pinned beneath a magnifying glass. Southern rays
Ignite the parchment of your manuscripts and
Damaged by their glare
I fall into a strange luminous blindness.

The shock value of your images
Remains unscathed by the brutal century
Since your death: your dishevelled corpse

On a blood-stained floor, your portrait –
Three strands of pearls wound tightly
Around your neck – on your murderer's wall.

Mostly it's your otherness that draws me
Into the maze of constellations. An obscure
Sense takes hold as if all along
A star, almost a soul, has hidden life from me.

We amass with blistered lips, parched tongues
To quench our thirst in the fountains of despair –
Virginia, Sylvia, Alfonsina and you, Delmira.

We lap at liquid lyrics. Your salt burns
Our wounds, sister, as your spirit rises
Engulfed by words that crackle and scorch.

I grasp the torch, present it heavenwards –
Oh, the indifference of the gods and poet men!
Your fame, the flame I brandish
Has it been caught in me like a brilliant butterfly?

More than your film noir demise, your words
Frighten. It's the claustrophobia you imparted
Enmeshed in the veil of a cruel world.

They wanted you demure, entrapped you, served
You up to feast on your spirit while you pleaded
With the star to share its light and forever veil your world.

Striking the rocks of your colliding metaphors
I ignite a spark to burn my manuscripts.
Will the flame surrender
Or in its halo of light have I been seized?

Amplitude

My ritual begins with brushing cobwebs
from the wall with our plaque, a trio of family
names, years born and buried. We never found
the words to sum them up. I rely on memory
to conjure empathy, grace, the twinkle
of a joke etched on each beloved face.

Ottawa's burial grounds, the acres
of hilly woods and gardens, prove sorrow
does fertilize well, graves carved to abide
from stones of the Laurentian Shield.
Among the phrases engraved by names
In loving memory wins a tally, *Always remembered*
a close second. I reach the meadow of lullabies
embedded with the tiniest plaques. Date of death
on Christmas Eve, she lived for 13 days.
Nearby, a boy, aged 4: *He was the stuff that dreams
are made of* alongside 2 angels and a bicycle.

I pass through the Beechwood gates
my sorrows small inside this amplitude of grief.

Only Known to God

we know why the junta
invaded on April 2, 1982
special forces backed by
conscripts plied with wine
then loaded semi-conscious and dispatched (no coats
or boots or proper training) to the bitter windy islands
the brutal diversion tactic to mitigate the junta's dying
days and we know why Thatcher dispatched her navy to land
7 weeks later with a fierce fight forcing the Argentine garrison to
surrender so she could win a second term
Las Malvinas son Argentinas /
The Falkland Islands are British
Soldado Argentino solo conocido por Dios /
Argentine Soldier only known to God
dear God we know
the deadly score
255 British soldiers to
649 Argentine recruits
but why can't you share
your divine knowledge
to say who are those
Argentines buried in the
cemetery in Darwin
the 123 graves marked
only known to you
or say who vandalized
the Virgin de Luján's head
and smashed her glass casing
January 2017 long after the futile war?

74

So Long, Rubin Carter

> *No one knows what freedom is*
> *But the lack of it killed that bird.*
> —Rubin Carter (1937-2014)

At a reading on writers in prison, a man wearing an Akubra
floats past my table. Nice hat, I say, and he sends a wink

my way as if he knows I'm nervous. He takes the stage
in his well-cut suit, the Akubra at a rakish tilt

and says, Sorry I'm not as good-looking as Denzel Washington.
Rubin Carter hovers on the stage all eloquence and dignity.

Float like a butterfly, Ali advised, sting like a bee,
but this Hurricane boxer understands humility. Grace

has long usurped his bitter rage. Rubin Carter spent
half of his twenty years in Trenton State in solitary

confinement, a place he called *the black hole of silence*.
No running water, five slices of stale bread per day

nothing to do but think and rage.
He fought hard for pencil and paper,

his lifeline out of hell,
and proclaimed his innocence.

Of his verse about a sparrow caged to death,
he wrote, *It is the only poem I have ever written*

as I'm sure is obvious to anyone who reads it.
No, Rubin Carter, the poem's a total knock-out.

So long, I say as you leave our stage for good.
So long: the words you knew too well.

We Do Not Want You to Die

For Theresa Spence, January 1, 2013

We want your strong voice
to fill our long, silent nights.
We do not want you to die.

We want to hear your voice carry
across the true north.
We do not want you to die.

We want the tyrants to listen
and end the injustice.
We do not want you to die.

We want to hear a new wisdom
emerge from your cry.
We do not want you to die.

We want to heal our green waters
and restore our blue woods.
We do not want you to die.

We want you to see a new dawn
and lead a new year.
We are many.
We do not want you to die.

Variations on April 9, 2017

Dance, dance, otherwise we have nothing.
    —Pina Bausch

You are born at 13:15 with my tendency
to arrive early but it's our ecstasy
you need to know about, the sashays
we all soft-shoed, brimming with crazy
love and life-affirming urgency!

I, your auntie, can't wait to blow
a blessing and trace a circle on your tiny palm.
How vast, how limitless the sense of grace
that this one tree, so often
           fractured and uprooted

endures and grows. You're the little branch
that holds a nest of songbirds who perch
and sing their chorus just for you! Yet deep
within your privilege lies the hope of dance
when you learn to walk this earth.

So you must know of this Sunday's
true realities: Refugees flee
with all they have left,
Sudanese line up for food,
Syrians kneel by their babies' graves
two days after the gassing.

By the time you're 30, I'll be among the family
dust in Beechwood Cemetery. Mix my ashes
with water – may there be some left for you.

Tikkun olam my Jewish friends have taught me
and you too must learn: to dance down storm,
behold things beautiful and not succumb –
      ricochet our love
      and go repair the world.

ESCAPE ROUTE

Equations

Already rattled by the 41-minute drive uphill on US-285,
the linear landscapes of dry-rigid New Mexican mesas
giving way to the Pajarito Plateau with incalculable

subdivisions, treeless house-clones with double
SUV-driveways, we stop at a Starbucks near the museum,
the drive-thru line-ups fissioning through the parking lot

in the 3 pm shift-change surge and it's even worse inside
as we inch forward behind twitchy types dressed in khakis
and golf shirts, pastel or striped, arms freckled or sunless,

and Contamination equals Leaching times Time so the longer
we wait the more our nervous systems absorb their thumb-flicks,
myopic cell-gazing, weight-shifting stances and tics, all suggesting

some inattention to detail an hour ago in their labs
setting in motion a time-sensitive trigger that any second now
will cause the whole damn place – 14,000 football fields in size –

to implode into a noxious cloud of dust, nuking
us here and now, all 9,000 physicists, engineers,
geoscientists, chemists plus contractors plus us two,

no worse than Hiroshima, Nagasaki – so if Cosmic Justice
equals Revenge divided by Time, some might say it's deserved
to die this way, skin peeling off, organs melting

and this is not my imagination on overdrive considering
the 2.2 pounds of plutonium that seem to have gone missing
and the 2,000 dumpsites contaminating this 43 square-mile

plateau, so yes, any nanosecond this could be IT,
death by human error caused by one caffeine-addicted
glitchy soul working at Los Alamos.

Neon

A harrowing americano later, having debated then dismissed
simply going back to Santa Fe, we swelter across the street
to our intended destination and the docent fixes on my pink

peace sign button worn for good luck and safety
with a forced smile, *Welcome to the Bradbury Science Museum!*
and ushers us hell bent towards the *peaceful innovations*

which really mean nuclear medicine like MRIs, *squeezing power
from pond scum* or nanotechnology, the science of the small,
and I'm disappointed to learn that the museum's name

has nothing to do with Ray but one Norris Bradbury,
the 2nd Los Alamos' director after Oppenheimer, and it's eerie
just us and the docent's perpetual smile as we move through dark

galleries on testing in the Nevada desert and *stockpile stewardship*
with 3D illustrations of elevator shafts boring into the earth's centre
to store the waste *safely* inside massive interlocking chambers

manipulated by robotics with offsite human guidance
which any thinking person would attribute to handling the worst
substances invented by disarming scientists who figure, hell!

might as well drill down by Vegas, gamblers and neon there anyway,
just your disposable losers, freak shows and impressionists
who could only benefit from a little continuous exposure,

and then the *proud history* of the Manhattan Project with replicas
of the first nuclear bombs sweetly named Little Boy and Fat Man
and the only thing I buy in the gift shop is a monograph

published by the venerable Los Alamos Historical Society
on Robert Oppenheimer, member of the secret group
created to construct the atom bomb, a New Yorker

known as Oppie to his friends, charged with treason
by McCarthy for being a Soviet agent but later cleared
who wrote of his atomic research *a great discovery*

*is a thing of beauty and knowledge is good
and good itself* so I have to wonder
about his mental health while standing here

in the *heart* of Los Alamos as the museum bills itself
with *over 70 years of innovation* and *leading
edge research* into WMDs.

Triumph equalling Heartlessness
the radiance of trophies
glowing on the dead.

Free Particle

Our museum closes at five, the docent sighs as if sorry
her workday is terminating while I clutch the monograph,
blurry-minded from quantum mechanics, free particles,

wave functions, harmonic oscillators. That's how the industry
operates, boggles politicians with proliferations of seemingly
innocuous factoids forming a supercritical mass of rock-hard

evidence hiding the gaps, unknowns and side effects
all undermined by campaign contributions and endowments
to harvest the brightest minds of America, like Oppie

the left-leaning Harvard fellow on some wartime
FBI custodial detention list (Arrest in the event of an attack!),
one of the *world's intellectual leaders*

who set up his lab here to shoot U-235
despite its unknown nuclear properties, plutonium in cyclotron
bombardment, the implosions tested in codenamed Trinity

(in unholy reference to Donne's sonnets) at Alamogordo,
July 16th on a jubilant 1945 night that had Oppie invoking
the Bhagavad Gita's *splendor of the mighty on*e

seen in *the radiance of a thousand stars* bursting in the sky,
calling himself *destroyer of worlds* but leaving the decision
to HS Truman who, within the month, deployed

Little Boy on Hiroshima followed 3 days later by Fat Man
on Nagasaki about which the monograph has but one paragraph
saying the attacks caused Los Alamos' scientists great sadness

so I have to get the hell out of hell and driving past the cloned
living quarters, I'm spinning like a free particle in a wave function
since at this point GW Bush is in charge and the devil

knows what he has in mind and none too soon we hit the highway
back to Santa Fe with its post-9/11 signage to follow a specific route
in case of evacuation, NOT to stop under any circumstances,

and I can't wait to get back to our little inn by the weeping willows
along the river in the artful town, to flee this place named after poplars
álamo blanco, álamo negro, álamo temblón repeated

as incantation past prickly slopes, the car rolling downhill
semi-conducted by Gravity plus Gas to the harmonic
álamo álamo álamo of our spinning wheels.

Evening Star

If art can be grounding, the next day I'm seeking terra firma
in the Santa Fe museum with its cubist terra-cotta walls
and docents who can tell with a glance they should leave me

alone as I spin through the galleries less attracted by canvasses
of calla lilies, zinnias and bleeding hearts in opulent flesh tones
than the primal red sky over blue land embracing light

in Evening Star No. VI which plays into the centrifuge
of my imagination as do constellations gazing upon
New York scrapers, night rectangles by haloed streetlights

or the Stieglitz photos depicting the artist's melancholy
smirk and Woolfesque drooping eyelids but my chain
reaction is triggered by Georgia O'Keeffe's desert

landscapes as I detect radioactive sludge glowing beneath
the blood-red rock formations of New Mexican mesas
while horned cow skulls collected in her Ghost Ranch

resemble painted icons of the great depression, droughtful
dust and possibly the artist's response to scientific doings
on the nearby Pajarito Plateau, dire warnings

of the consequences of betraying laws of nature
considering O'Keeffe put down her paintbrush
when her eyes faded (did she know the linkage

of macular degeneration to atomic blast exposure?)
and Oppenheimer died of throat cancer
and his daughter later committed suicide

at 31 after she was banned from working as a UN
translator because of her dead father's questionable
security risk, flecks of truth that build into a cosmic

shower as I spin a pathway through the galleries,
an escape route radiated by the nano-
beauty of a numbered evening star.

CITY MISCREANTS

I try to apply colours
like words that shape poems,
like notes that shape music.
I make no distinction between poetry and painting.
—Joan Miró

Raspberry

You gotta beware of thorns
        when you're picking in thickets
swallow the sour and hard
        with the ripe and the soft
cry when you have to
stick out your tongue
give lip when you're squeamish
spit out   seeds that get stuck in your teeth

you gotta play
        separate instruments
gotta have your own spoon
whip up some folderol
make it froth   pink and crunchy

you gotta laugh at his jokes
        'cause he laughs at yours
gotta face the music
disavow psychobabble   (*long term
relationship* sounds like a prison sentence)
replace repetition   the hateful routine
show grace when you lose
        the inevitable skirmish

you gotta flimflam the truth
           tickle the foam
rinse your own berries
           pretend cream and sugar
let him rummage alone   go sit
at the table be patient and wait

Flimflam Cycle (aka One-Worders for an Imaginary Conversation)

Welcome to our nation's capital	Flimflam
Isn't that a place in Manitoba?	Flin-Flon
Diplomats speaking out	Immunity
Parliamentarians speaking out	Impunity
Who was that masked man?	Harper
Spokesperson for multinational oil	Flimflammer
Welcome to the world's largest collection of lie detectors	Flimflamier
The liberation of accepting you're bad at something	Ukulele
Don't worry, I'm a professional	Fuck-up
Your heartbeat when you meet your lover	Iamb
Your heartbeat at the breakup	Spondee
The post-post-postmodern canon	Flimfragmentation
What's most important, reading or writing?	Yes
Tip for being a decent writer	Rewrite
Tip for being a decent reciter	Elocution
How do you get your ideas?	Acrobatics
Rumours of demise greatly exaggerated	Poetry
One-word poems with lengthy titles	Flimflamiestest

Vermillion

We're slow setting out
from Puerto Vallarta
in the yellow kayak   with red stripes
my paddle whiplashing   Bahía de Banderas
as the bobbing convoy recedes ahead of us
a distancing rainbow on the blue-green seas.

Stuffed into life jackets
for the deepest of Pacific bays
our excursion involves thousands
of dips and pulls   – right and up,
left and up   right and up again –
towards an isolated cove.

I'm surprised at the soundlessness
of the endeavour   just a few stray seabirds
gossiping overhead   and the awkward smack
of my paddle when it doesn't slice the sea
as it should.   I should have noted how noiseless
his efforts behind me   in our kayak
but I'm all aching shoulders   and bruised pride
as we come in last   from the long, hard crossing.

The kayak almost tips   when I get out and pull us ashore
avoiding eye contact with the Mexican guide
who points us up towards the others
        already clambering the jungly hills.

The path is mossy   humid   dark
slopes gently then rises vertically
into a tropical microclimate.   Clusters
of giant ferns splay out in symmetrical
bouquets   twice my height   a frenzied
mass of curlicue leaves.

And trees the likes of which I've never seen
their gnarly trunks twist and turn
tall as a herd of woeful elephants
shaking their heads   no   in the altitudinal
breeze.   The guide points out the orchids
barely visible within   slanting shafts of light
their baby fingers of scarlet and mauve
some spotted   tiger-striped
and it turns out these are parasites
leaching onto trees   to suck their nutrients.
More than a symbiotic relationship
the orchid thrives on another's energy.

After the hike and tortillas, we drink
Dos Equis on the beach   a fair distance from the others
in our typical not-quite-fitting-in stance.

He snorkels while I sit in the sand
and watch the back of his white T-shirt
surveying the depths   like a benevolent shark.
Every half hour or so he flipper-walks
back to me with a shell or sea urchin
that he offers as a gift   then returns to his
obsession with the sea. I can sense he's happy
out there and I'm happy too which is a relief

because if you can't find happiness
in the bountiful microclimate   of a Pacific cove
you'll never find it   anywhere.

Later he waddles back, kicks off his flippers
gives me a salty kiss and places in my palm
a small translucent stone, its oval surface layered
        with vermillion filaments.

The sun is just an inch or so over the horizon
when we set off into headwinds
and damned if we're going to be last again
I work my paddle in fast muscular thrusts
closing in on the others   proud to demonstrate
that we too   are competent at this endeavour.

Just when our kayak passes the sleek blue
vessel containing an American couple, the woman
in front says, *You know, he's not even
paddling*, and I whip around   see him
languishing   paddle on his knees
grinning at me   and you'd never know
he'd just given me his heart.

Me: Why aren't you paddling?
Him: You're doing great by yourself.

Goldenrod

After reciting the fine print
on the French's Classic label
I segue into a diatribe
on how I'm allergic to goldenrod
egg whites but not egg yolks
and isn't this the yoke of destiny
to hide behind shades like I do
and pretend to be by myself
when I'm really not and
that's the whole point

to feel as real and integrated
together as alone and all this
is too much unfiltered thought
so I refrain from saying
it's ok to do the paddling
if I know you've got my back
because you laugh at my jokes
and you listen. When he leans
across the table and asks
it's easy to answer the truth.

Him: Are you allergic to me?
Me: Never!

City Miscreants

Setting off   from the dock in upstate New York
the waters seem calm enough   as we paddle across the lake
slow to recognize   the blue-grey watercolors of a Turner storm
churning on the horizon   as errant sunrays escape low-lying clouds.

I should've known the deeper story can only be discerned
by plunging   beneath the surface
but sitting stern   I boast about learning to right a tipped
canoe at summer camp   turning back from time to time
to spot our receding plot of sumac and ferns
bordering the ochre cottage
a bargain summer rental enabled by proximity
to the maximum security prison
where our surly neighbours work.

The siren for a midday prison ritual resounds
to chase the loitering swallows.   An interval
pausing violins in an overture of *Sturm und Drang*
then a gust rams our canoe   to flip us into
an assault of cold.
             I struggle   flailing
          deeper
                     deeper …

Impulse kicks in   my head finds air and reason.
He is gone.   I see no artful light
as whitecaps somersault   across the murkiest canvas.
Riding the waves, our paddles drift
away …

The lake and all is quiet   a drenching loneliness
                    until at last
his panicked eyes   bob up.

We tread water   holding onto the canoe
seconds   minutes   maybe hours
to the magic of a sound   we once disdained.

An outboard motor   buzzes   towards us
driven by a man   enjoying a tuna
sandwich by his window
when he spotted two idiots
capsized   in the middle   of the lake.

During the rescue
I see us through his eyes
city miscreants   almost in tears
profusely grateful for wool blankets and   rope to tow
the waterlogged canoe.

Our guardian   retired from Dannemora Prison
just last May knows the ochre cottage
leaves us at the dock without a farewell
wave   as if we've survived some test
                not with flying colours
but a passing grade.

After hot showers   shots of Southern Comfort
the evensong of swallows returning to skim the lake
draws us out onto the lawn
where vespertine fireflies dart

among the sumac and
the broad triangulated fronds
baptized Sensitive Ferns.

We play killer croquet.
He's cobalt to my red.   It's tricky
factoring in the slope   to whack the ball
          through shadowy hoops
with accuracy.   I'm already
dancing my victory jive
when he aces a long shot.   His ball whacks mine.
He swings his mallet   sends my red splashing into the lake
          swings again
cobalt soars   beyond the dock

while the angel in disguise
lurks beyond the clearing   eyes ablaze
with well-earned mockery.

Go Back to Finger Painting

After Paul Klee's Architecture of the Plain, *1923*

Remember the smeary freedom and tactile bliss? How you could fill the page as it curled with fire and became uniquely yours, cobalt never just cobalt and red never lonely red.

The fluidity of identities, a meld of hues and primaries, of places, lands and waters crossed, capsized emotions. Light and its absence, the greatest sorrows, fragmented and unpredictable. By the time you finger your colour it's already changed.

Take Klee whose watercolours shift according to your gaze. His Architecture of the Plain depends on conjecture. Some days deliver its pleasing synchronicity – darker blues and greens defining margins left and right – and the coloured rectangles overlap, now raspberry, now vermillion. Fleeting moments pass and all you see is collision, hear a noisy argument, colours clamouring for space.

Klee knew what he was doing – flat as a checked shirt pressed on an ironing board, yet there's such depth to the painting, you want to put your hand through the paper and feel around, you want to wear your shades, tag your name graffiti-style to the lowest rainbow stripe.

This is a multicoloured manifesto of love. Darkness and
light in perfect Greek proportionality, an artful construction
based on math and spontaneity where form is all there
without being too visible.

Look carefully: the ratio of the smaller part (the cobalts, say)
to the larger part (the reds) equals the ratio of the larger part
to the entirety (the painting). Even your fleeting childhood,
even your fingers painting reflect a perfect symmetry where
> cobalt is to red
>
> equals red is to (cobalt plus red).

See what I mean?
The painting is greater than the sum of its brushstrokes.

Notes

The title of this book is taken from a line in the poem, "Angel," by Alexander Pushkin, translated by Yevgeny Bonver.

The epigraph to "Origins of the Blast" is from the poem "Godzilla in Mexico" by Roberto Bolaño in *The Romantic Dogs* (translated by Laura Healy, New Directions, 2008).

The Robert Thomas epigraph to "Listen, Heart" is from his poem "Catchy Tunes" published in *Poetry*, July/August 2013.

The inspiration for "Mirror Princess" comes from F*or a Romantic Fantasy*, a 2015 installation by Stephanie Loveless at Fonderie Darling. The sound piece emitted a chorus of female voices replicating time-stretched recordings of the 1937 Walt Disney song, "Some Day My Prince Will Come."

"The Dial-a-Poem Poets" refers to the 1980 album, *Sugar, Alcohol & Meat,* with its cover art by Robert Mapplethorpe, presented at the Montreal Museum of Fine Arts during the 2016/2017 exhibition, *Focus: Perfection – Robert Mapplethorpe.*

The citations quoted in "Woman of Two Million Names" refer to the following poets and their works:
Mary di Michele, "The Mountain after Klein" from *The Montreal Book of the Dead* (Vallum Chapbook Series No. 17, 2014).
Nicole Brossard, "16" from *A Tilt in the Wondering* (Vallum Chapbook Series No. 15, 2013.)

Hélène Dorion, "Temps, traces" from *Autour du temps – Anthologies de poètes québécois contemporains* (Éditions du Noroît, 1997).

Robyn Sarah, "Mile End, April into June" from *Pause for Breath* (Biblioasis, 2009).

Carmine Starnino, "Squash Rackets" from *The Best Canadian Poetry in English* (Tightrope Books, 2008.)

Sina Queyras, "Over to You" from *MxT* (Coach House Books, 2014).

The epigraph to "High Beams" is from *Theory of Colours* (1810) by Johann Wolfgang Goethe (translated by Charles Lock Eastlake in 1840, MIT Press, 1970), a foundational source of inspiration for this book.

The glosa, "Sister," is after a poem by Delmira Agustini, the Uruguayan poet (1886-1914) killed by her ex-husband in a murder-suicide. The lines cited are from *Selected Poetry of Delmira Agustini – Poetics of Eros,* edited and translated by Alejandro Cáceres (Southern Illinois University Press, 2003).

"So Long, Rubin Carter" is a tribute to the boxer and advocate for prisoners' rights. The epigraph is from *The Eye of the Hurricane: My Path from Darkness to Freedom* by Rubin Carter with Ken Klonsky (Chicago Review Press, 2011).

The poem, "We Do Not Want You to Die," was delivered to Theresa Spence, elder from Attawapiskat First Nation, during her hunger strike on Victoria Island in the Ottawa River.

Acknowledgements

I would like to thank the editors of the magazines where earlier versions of certain poems and sequences first appeared, including *Bywords* ("Across the Condiments"), *Montréal Serai* ("Red on Red"), *Literary Review of Canada* ("Note to a Mapless Self"), *The Night Heron Barks* ("Rose Juggler"), *Arc Poetry* ("Escape Route"), and *The Ekphrastic Review* ("Go Back to Finger Painting").

Muchas gracias to *Confabulario, Suplemento cultural, El Universal* in Mexico for publishing Spanish versions of "Go into the Dark," "Coming Home," and the sequence "Sinville" all translated by the phenomenal Argentine writer Marina Porcelli.

Special thanks to sensitivity reader Curran Katsi'sóro:kwas Jacobs of Kahnawake for her careful review of the "Sinville" sequence and "We Do Not Want You to Die."

Thanks also to Jan Jorgensen for including "Here They Are!" in the chapbook, *My Island My City* (d'Iberville Press, 2019).

I'm very grateful to Michael Mirolla, Connie McParland and the team at Guernica Editions for their support and diligence in bringing this book to life. Deep gratitude to Elana Wolff for her astute editing and brilliant poetics.

Heartfelt thanks to my family, especially Henry Alexander Siré whose birth inspired "Variations on April 9, 2017."

This book is dedicated to my beloved Otokar with our motto: *amor & cachondeo* (loosely translated as 'love & shenanigans'). His sense of humour and generosity of spirit in enduring my relentless scrutiny are epic.

About the Author

Cora Siré lives in Montreal where she writes poetry, fiction and essays. She is the author of a debut poetry collection, *Signs of Subversive Innocents*. Her poems have appeared in magazines such as *Arc Poetry*, *Literary Review of Canada*, *Geist*, *Montréal Serai*, *The Ekphrastic Review*, *The Night Heron Barks* (U.S.) and *Confabulario* (Mexico) as well as in anthologies including *Another Dysfunctional Cancer Poem Anthology* and *The Best Canadian Poetry in English 2009*. Her novel, *The Other Oscar*, was shortlisted for Quattro Books' Ken Klonsky Novella Contest in 2015 and was recently translated into French as *Radeau*. Her second novel, *Behold Things Beautiful*, was a finalist for the Quebec Writers' Federation Paragraphe Hugh MacLennan Prize for Fiction in 2017. Author website: www.quena.ca.

MIX
Paper from
responsible sources
FSC
www.fsc.org
FSC® C100212

Printed in February 2021
by Gauvin Press,
Gatineau, Québec